I0846135

SAVE YOUR BRAIN

Steps and strategies to help boost your cognitive functions and reduce decline

Oprah Reginald

Copyright © 2023 by Oprah Reginald

No portion of this publication may be reproduced, distributed, or communicated in any form, whether by photocopying, recording, or other mechanical or electronic means, without the publisher's prior written authorization with the exception of brief quotations used in critical reviews and other non-commercial uses allowed by copyright law.

TABLE OF CONTENTS

brain and is responsible for connecting the cerebrum and cerebellum to the spinal cord. It regulates essential functions like breathing, heart rate, blood pressure, digestion, and sleep-wake cycles.			37

7. Cerebellum: Situated at the back of the brain, it is responsible for coordinating voluntary movements, maintaining balance, and posture.			37

8. Thalamus: An important relay station in the brain, it receives sensory information from various parts of the body and routes it to the appropriate areas of the cerebral cortex for processing.			37

9. Hypothalamus: Involved in regulating body temperature, hunger, thirst, sleep, emotions, and controlling the pituitary gland to manage hormone secretion.			37

10. Limbic System: A group of interconnected structures, including the hippocampus, amygdala, and hypothalamus, which play a significant role in memory, emotions, motivation, and learning.			37

11. Hippocampus: Vital for forming new memories and spatial navigation.			37

12. Amygdala: responsible for processing emotions like aggression and fear.			38

13. Pituitary Gland: A small endocrine gland located at the base of the brain, it controls various hormonal secretions and regulates bodily functions			38

14. Corpus Callosum: A broad band of nerve fibers that connects the left and right

ranging from 60-80%. It is characterized by the buildup of abnormal protein structures in the brain, known as amyloid plaques and tau tangles. These plaques and tangles interfere with communication between brain cells, leading to their dysfunction and eventual death. 50

2. Vascular Dementia: This type of dementia is caused by reduced blood flow to the brain, leading to the death of brain cells. It can occur after a stroke or due to other blood vessel-related problems, such as small vessel disease or blood vessel blockages. 50

3. Lewy Body Dementia: This condition is caused by the presence of abnormal protein deposits called Lewy bodies in the brain. These deposits disrupt the normal functioning of brain cells and affect cognitive abilities, motor skills, and behavior. 50

4. Frontotemporal Dementia (FTD): FTD is characterized by damage to the frontal and temporal lobes of the brain. The exact cause is not always known, but it is associated with the buildup of abnormal proteins, genetic mutations, or other unknown factors. 51

5. Mixed Dementia: Some individuals may have a combination of more than one type of dementia, such as Alzheimer's disease and vascular dementia. The coexistence of multiple factors can complicate the symptoms and diagnosis. 51

6. Creutzfeldt-Jakob Disease (CJD): This is a rare and fatal prion disease that causes

stimulates neuroplasticity, the brain's ability to reorganize and form new neural connections. This can enhance cognitive reserve, making the brain more resilient against neurological diseases like dementia. 62

4. Reduction of Risk Factors: Exercise helps manage cardiovascular risk factors like hypertension, diabetes, and obesity. These conditions are linked to an increased risk of dementia, and exercise can reduce their impact on the brain.   62

5. Decreased Inflammation: Regular exercise reduces chronic inflammation, which can contribute to cognitive decline. Lower inflammation levels protect brain cells and support their proper functioning.   63

6. Antioxidant Effects: Exercise enhances the body's production of antioxidants, which combat oxidative stress. Oxidative stress can damage brain cells and contribute to dementia, but regular exercise helps mitigate this effect.   63

7. Enhanced Brain-Derived Neurotrophic Factor (BDNF): Exercise increases the production of BDNF, a protein that supports the growth and survival of brain cells. Higher BDNF levels have been associated with better cognitive function and reduced risk of dementia.   63

8. Stress Reduction: Physical activity helps alleviate stress, which can negatively impact brain health. Managing stress through exercise supports a healthier brain.   63

4. Comprehensive Evaluation: The specialist will conduct a comprehensive evaluation, which may include a thorough medical history, cognitive tests, neurological examination, blood tests, brain imaging (e.g., MRI or CT scan), and sometimes lumbar puncture (spinal tap) to rule out other possible causes of cognitive impairment. 81

5. Medical History and Symptoms: During the evaluation, the doctor will inquire about your medical history, family history of dementia, and details about the symptoms you've been experiencing. 81

6. Cognitive Testing: Various tests will be administered to assess memory, attention, language, problem-solving skills, and other cognitive functions. 81

7. Neurological Examination: The doctor will perform a neurological examination to check for any physical signs of brain abnormalities. 81

8. Brain Imaging: Brain imaging, such as MRI or CT scan, can help identify brain changes associated with different types of dementia and exclude other conditions that might mimic dementia. 81

9. Blood Tests: Blood tests can help identify underlying medical conditions that might contribute to cognitive decline, such as vitamin deficiencies, thyroid problems, or infections. 82

10. Lumbar Puncture (Spinal Tap): In certain cases, a lumbar puncture may be

regulate your body's internal clock, known as the circadian rhythm, which is closely linked to sleep quality.   86

3. Have a Comfortable Bedtime Routine: Establish a consistent and comfortable routine before bedtime for your body to adapt to it. Activities like reading a book, meditating, or taking a warm bath can promote relaxation and better sleep.   86

4. Limit Daytime Naps: While short power naps can be beneficial, excessive daytime sleep can disrupt your nighttime sleep. Keep naps to a maximum of 20-30 minutes and avoid napping too close to bedtime.   87

5. Manage Exposure to Light: Light exposure can affect your circadian rhythm. During the day, get natural sunlight, and in the evening, reduce exposure to bright screens, such as smartphones and tablets, as the blue light emitted can interfere with your ability to fall asleep.   87

6. Be Mindful of Diet and Exercise: Regular physical activity and a balanced diet can positively impact your sleep and overall brain health. Avoid heavy meals and caffeine close to bedtime, as they may disrupt your sleep patterns.   88

7. Limit Alcohol and Nicotine: Both alcohol and nicotine can negatively affect sleep quality. Try to limit or avoid their consumption, especially in the hours leading up to bedtime.   88

8. Make your Sleep Environment Friendly: Ensure that your bedroom is set up in such

women, as age is a significant risk factor for developing dementia. 92

2. Risk Factors: Both men and women share some common risk factors for dementia, such as age, family history, and genetics. However, certain risk factors may impact each gender differently. For example, cardiovascular risk factors like high blood pressure and cholesterol may have a stronger association with dementia in men. 92

3. Types of Dementia: Alzheimer's disease is the most common form of dementia in both genders. However, some studies indicate that women may be more susceptible to Alzheimer's, while men may have a slightly higher risk of developing other types of dementia, like vascular dementia. 93

4. Cognitive Decline: Although the overall pattern of cognitive decline is similar in men and women with dementia, some studies suggest that women may experience more severe cognitive impairment in the early stages of the disease. 93

5. Psychosocial Aspects: The experience of dementia can also differ between men and women due to societal norms and gender roles. Women often bear a higher caregiving burden as they are more likely to be caregivers for family members with dementia. 93

6. Hormonal Influences: Hormonal changes throughout a woman's life, such as during menopause, may play a role in cognitive

3. Genetics: Some genetic factors are
associated with an increased risk of
developing dementia. The apolipoprotein E
(APOE) gene, specifically the APOE-ε4
allele, is a significant genetic risk factor for
Alzheimer's disease, the most common form
of dementia. Studies have suggested that

women may have a higher prevalence of this genetic risk factor compared to men. 97

4. Cardiovascular Health: Cardiovascular risk factors such as hypertension, diabetes, and high cholesterol are linked to an increased risk of dementia. Women tend to have a higher prevalence of certain cardiovascular risk factors, which could contribute to their higher dementia risk. 98

5. Social and Lifestyle Factors: Women often take on caregiving roles for family members with dementia, leading to increased stress and potential negative impacts on their own health. Additionally, certain lifestyle choices, such as diet, exercise, and education, can influence dementia risk, and these factors may vary between genders. 98

6. Underdiagnosis in Men: Dementia symptoms can manifest differently in men and women. Men may be more likely to exhibit aggressive or disruptive behaviors, leading to a higher likelihood of being diagnosed with other conditions, such as depression or behavioral disorders, instead of dementia. 98

7. Cerebrovascular Differences: Some studies suggest that women may have a higher incidence of cerebrovascular disease, such as small vessel disease, which can contribute to cognitive impairment and vascular dementia. 99

8. Neurobiological Differences: Research has shown that male and female brains differ in their structure and function, which

modifications, and strategies to manage
behavioral symptoms.   103

3. Education and Support: Dementia
experts play an essential role in educating
patients and their families about the
condition. They provide information on
disease progression, coping strategies, and
ways to enhance the quality of life for those
living with dementia.   103

4. Caregiver Training: Supporting caregivers
is a crucial aspect of dementia care. Experts
offer training to caregivers, helping them
understand the challenges associated with
dementia and equipping them with the skills
to provide appropriate care and support. 104

5. Psychological Support: Dementia can
take an emotional toll on both patients and
caregivers. Experts offer psychological
support to help individuals cope with the
stress, anxiety, and depression that may
accompany the disease.   104

6. Medication Management: Dementia
experts are knowledgeable about various
medications used to manage dementia
symptoms. They monitor patients'
responses to medications and make
adjustments as needed.   104

7. Research and Clinical Trials: Many
dementia experts are involved in research
to advance knowledge about dementia
causes, treatments, and potential cures.
They may participate in clinical trials to test
new therapies and interventions.   104

8. Promoting Independence: Dementia

experts work with patients to promote independence for as long as possible. They develop strategies to enhance daily living skills and support autonomy while ensuring safety.   105

9. Advocacy and Policy Development: Some experts on dementia are actively involved in advocating for better policies and resources to support individuals with dementia and their families. They work to raise awareness and reduce stigma surrounding the condition.   105

10. Community Engagement: Dementia experts often engage with the community to educate the public about dementia, early warning signs, and the importance of seeking early diagnosis and intervention. 105

11. End-of-life Care: Dementia experts support patients and their families in making end-of-life decisions and ensuring that their wishes are respected.   105

CONCLUSION   108

In conclusion, dementia is a complex and debilitating neurological condition that poses significant challenges to affected individuals, their families, and society at large. Throughout this discussion, we have explored the various aspects of dementia, including its definition, causes, symptoms, and impact on individuals' cognitive and functional abilities.   108

INTRODUCTION

Once upon a time, in the vast realm of human biology, there existed a remarkable organ known as the brain. Hidden within the protective confines of the skull, this enigmatic structure held the key to human consciousness, intelligence, and emotions. It was the central character in the fascinating saga of the human mind, orchestrating every thought, memory, and action that shaped the lives of individuals and shaped the course of humanity.

At the heart of our story, the brain was a complex and intricate network of billions of nerve cells called neurons, each connected through a web of pathways that transmitted electrical signals. These signals, like stars in the night sky, formed mesmerizing constellations of neural patterns that governed our thoughts and decisions. The brain's labyrinthine architecture intrigued scientists and philosophers alike, compelling them to unravel its mysteries and unlock its potential.

As the story unfolded, the brain's incredible ability to adapt and change, known as neuroplasticity, took center stage. This remarkable quality allowed it to learn from experiences, shaping and reshaping its connections to accommodate new knowledge and skills. Like a skilled artist, it painted the canvas of human cognition, creating masterpieces of innovation and creativity.

Yet, the brain also faced its share of challenges. It encountered storms of stress and storms of emotions, each capable of altering its delicate equilibrium. These tempests threatened to disrupt the harmony within, but the brain displayed resilience and determination, weathering the storms with grace and courage.

In the tale of the brain, emotions played a vital role. Joy, sorrow, love, and fear painted vivid colors on the canvas of human existence. The brain's emotional center, the amygdala, acted as both a guardian and a conductor of these emotions, guiding their flow and allowing us to experience the kaleidoscope of feelings that defined our humanity.

As the narrative progressed, the brain's ceaseless pursuit of understanding its own mysteries gave birth to fields of neuroscience and psychology. These scholarly adventurers embarked on a quest to decipher the enigmatic codes of cognition and the intricate dance of neurotransmitters that influenced our perceptions and behaviors.

In the midst of this unfolding epic, the brain found itself intertwined with technology. From the invention of the earliest tools to the dawn of artificial intelligence, this partnership between the organic and the artificial reshaped the destiny of humankind, birthing a new era of possibilities and ethical dilemmas.

With every turn of the page, the story of the brain presented a captivating tale of resilience, curiosity, and the human spirit's indomitable will. It reminded us that despite our vast knowledge, we had only scratched the surface of its potential. The brain remained a universe waiting to be fully explored, promising to reveal astonishing secrets and expand the boundaries of human comprehension.

As we close this prologue, the journey of the brain continues to unfold, with countless chapters yet to be written. It is a saga of wonder and exploration, a story that has shaped humanity and, in turn, been shaped by it. The brain, the protagonist of this epic tale, stands as a testament to the human quest for understanding, and it invites us to be active participants in the adventure of unlocking the hidden wonders of our own minds.

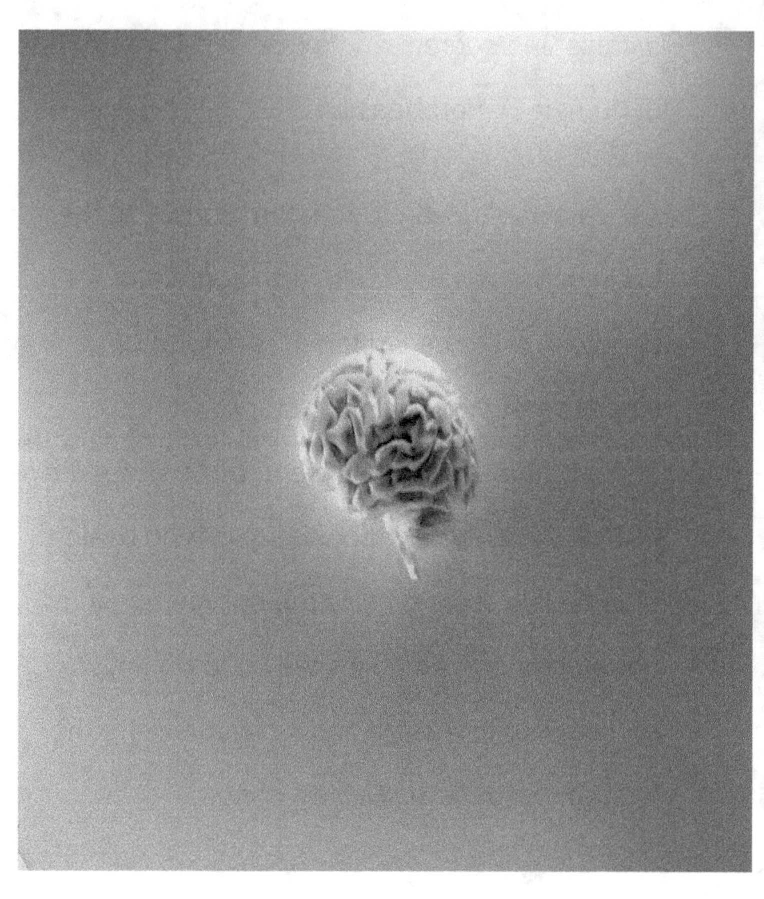

CHAPTER ONE

MEANING, COMPONENTS AND THEIR FUNCTIONS:

The brain is the central organ of the nervous system which plays a vital role in processing and interpreting information from the body's senses. It is responsible for controlling various functions, including thoughts, emotions, memories, and movements.

Here are the major components of the brain and their functions;

1. **Cerebrum:** This is the largest part of the brain that is divided into two. (left and right) hemispheres . It plays a critical role in conscious thought, voluntary movements, sensory perception, and language processing.
2. **Frontal Lobe**: Located at the front of the cerebrum, it is involved in decision-making, problem-solving, planning, personality, and emotional regulation.
3. **Parietal Lobe:** Positioned behind the frontal lobe, it processes sensory information, such as touch, temperature, pain, and spatial awareness.
4. **Occipital Lobe:** Found at the back of the cerebrum, it primarily handles visual processing and interpretation.
5. **Temporal Lobe:** Situated on the sides of the cerebrum, it plays a crucial role in hearing, language comprehension, memory consolidation, and emotional responses.

6. **Brainstem:** located at the base of the brain and is responsible for connecting the cerebrum and cerebellum to the spinal cord. It regulates essential functions like breathing, heart rate, blood pressure, digestion, and sleep-wake cycles.
7. **Cerebellum**: Situated at the back of the brain, it is responsible for coordinating voluntary movements, maintaining balance, and posture.
8. **Thalamus:** An important relay station in the brain, it receives sensory information from various parts of the body and routes it to the appropriate areas of the cerebral cortex for processing.
9. **Hypothalamus**: Involved in regulating body temperature, hunger, thirst, sleep, emotions, and controlling the pituitary gland to manage hormone secretion.
10. **Limbic System:** A group of interconnected structures, including the hippocampus, amygdala, and hypothalamus, which play a significant role in memory, emotions, motivation, and learning.

11. **Hippocampus:** Vital for forming new memories and spatial navigation.
12. **Amygdala:** responsible for processing emotions like aggression and fear.
13. **Pituitary Gland**: A small endocrine gland located at the base of the brain, it controls various hormonal secretions and regulates bodily functions
14. **Corpus Callosum:** A broad band of nerve fibers that connects the left and right hemispheres which allow communication and gathering of information between them.

These components work together in a highly interconnected manner to facilitate cognitive processes, emotional responses, sensory perception, and the overall regulation of bodily functions. It's important to note that brain function is a highly intricate and ongoing field of research, and new discoveries may continue to enhance our understanding of the brain's complexities.

CHAPTER TWO

CHANGES AS THE BRAIN AGES:

The aging brain is a complex topic that involves various changes and challenges as individuals grow older. As we age, our brain undergoes a natural process of physiological and functional changes. These changes can affect cognition, memory, attention, and overall brain health. Let's delve into some insights.

1. **Structural Changes:** One of the noticeable changes in the aging brain is the reduction in brain volume. The brain tends to shrink slightly with age, particularly in regions associated with memory and cognitive functions which is known as brain atrophy.

2. **Neural Connections:** As people age, there may be a decline in the number of neural connections and synapses, which are crucial for information processing and communication within the brain.

3. **Neurotransmitters:** The production and regulation of neurotransmitters, the chemicals responsible for transmitting signals between nerve cells, can also be affected by aging. Some neurotransmitter levels, such as dopamine and serotonin, may decrease, influencing mood and cognitive processes.

4. **Memory:** Age-related changes can impact different types of memory. While older adults may experience difficulty with episodic memory (remembering specific events), semantic memory (general knowledge) tends to be more preserved.

5. **Cognitive Functions:** Aging can lead to a decline in certain cognitive functions, such as processing speed, attention, and executive functions like problem-solving and multitasking.

6. **Neuroplasticity:** Although the aging brain experiences some decline, it still possesses a degree of neuroplasticity, the ability to reorganize and adapt to new experiences and learning. Engaging in mentally stimulating activities and lifelong learning can help maintain cognitive function.

7. **Risk Factors:** Certain factors can accelerate age-related cognitive decline. These include genetics, lifestyle choices (diet, physical activity, smoking), chronic health conditions (diabetes, hypertension), and social engagement.

8. **Neurodegenerative Problems:** The
   possibilities of neurodegenerative
   problems, such as Alzheimer's and
   Parkinson's, increases as we age.
   These conditions are characterized by
   progressive deterioration of brain
   function and can have significant
   impacts on an individual's life.

9. **Protective Factors**: Some factors
   may promote healthy brain aging.
   Regular physical exercise, a balanced
   diet rich in antioxidants and omega-3
   fatty acids, social interaction, and
   mentally stimulating activities can
   contribute to maintaining cognitive
   health.

10. **Cognitive Reserve:** Cognitive reserve
    refers to the brain's ability to cope with
    brain damage or age-related changes
    while maintaining cognitive function.
    High cognitive reserve, often associated
    with education and lifelong learning, can
    offer a protective effect against cognitive
    decline.

In conclusion, the aging brain is subject to
several changes that can affect cognitive

abilities and brain health. However, adopting a healthy lifestyle, staying mentally active, and engaging in brain-stimulating activities can contribute to better cognitive function and overall well-being in later life. Regular check-ups and early detection of cognitive issues are essential for managing age-related brain changes and promoting healthy aging.

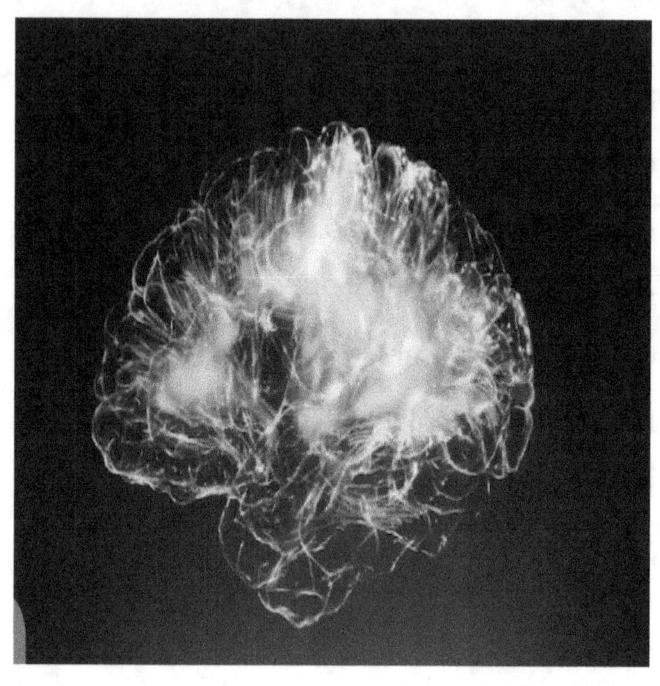

CHAPTER THREE

INTRODUCTION TO DEMENTIA:

Dementia is a broad term used to describe a group of cognitive disorders characterized by a decline in memory, thinking, reasoning, and the ability to perform daily activities. It is an ailment that comes as a result of different kinds of underlying brain problems . Alzheimer's disease happens to have the highest rank like 60-80% when it comes to the cause of dementia.

Other causes of dementia include vascular dementia, Lewy body dementia, frontotemporal dementia, and others. Each type of dementia presents with distinct symptoms and progression patterns.

The early stages of dementia may involve mild forgetfulness and difficulty finding words, but as the condition progresses, individuals may experience severe memory loss, confusion, and changes in behavior and personality.

Risk factors for dementia include advanced age, family history of the condition, cardiovascular risk factors, and certain genetic mutations. Although there is no cure for most forms of dementia, early diagnosis and appropriate management can help improve quality of life and delay the progression of symptoms.

Supportive care, medications, and therapies tailored to the individual's needs are essential components of dementia management. It's crucial for both affected individuals and their caregivers to seek professional support and resources to cope with the challenges of this condition. Research and ongoing efforts continue to explore potential treatments and better understanding of dementia to improve its

management and enhance the lives of those

affected.

CAUSES OF DEMENTIA:

Let's delve into some of the causes of

dementia

1. **Alzheimer's Disease**: Happens to have the highest rank in the cause of dementia ranging from 60-80%. It is characterized by the buildup of abnormal protein structures in the brain, known as amyloid plaques and tau tangles. These plaques and tangles interfere with communication between brain cells, leading to their dysfunction and eventual death.

2. **Vascular Dementia:** This type of dementia is caused by reduced blood flow to the brain, leading to the death of brain cells. It can occur after a stroke or due to other blood vessel-related problems, such as small vessel disease or blood vessel blockages.

3. **Lewy Body Dementia**: This condition is caused by the presence of abnormal protein deposits called Lewy bodies in the brain. These deposits disrupt the normal functioning of brain cells and affect cognitive abilities, motor skills, and behavior.

4. **Frontotemporal Dementia (FTD):**
    FTD is characterized by damage to the
    frontal and temporal lobes of the brain.
    The exact cause is not always known,
    but it is associated with the buildup of
    abnormal proteins, genetic mutations, or
    other unknown factors.

5. **Mixed Dementia:** Some individuals
    may have a combination of more than
    one type of dementia, such as
    Alzheimer's disease and vascular
    dementia. The coexistence of multiple
    factors can complicate the symptoms
    and diagnosis.

6. **Creutzfeldt-Jakob Disease (CJD):**
    This is a rare and fatal prion disease
    that causes rapid deterioration of brain
    function. It is believed to be caused by
    abnormal proteins called prions, which
    trigger a chain reaction of protein
    misfolding in the brain.

7. **Huntington's Disease:** This is an
    inherited genetic disorder caused by a
    mutation in the huntingtin gene. The
    mutation leads to the production of
    abnormal proteins, which gradually
    damage brain cells, particularly in the
    basal ganglia and cerebral cortex.

8. **Normal Pressure Hydrocephalus (NPH):** NPH happens when too much cerebrospinal fluid builds up in the brain's ventricles and thereby being the reason for brain tissue being compressed and destroyed. The exact cause of NPH is often unknown, but it may result from infection, head injury, or bleeding in the brain.

It's important to note that some causes of dementia are reversible if treated promptly, such as certain infections, metabolic disorders, and medication side effects. Early detection and appropriate management can make a significant difference in the outcome for these cases. If you or someone you know is experiencing symptoms of dementia, it is crucial to seek medical evaluation and support.

CHAPTER FOUR

INSIGHTS ON ALZHEIMER'S DISEASE:

Alzheimer's disease is a progressive neurodegenerative disorder that primarily affects the brain, leading to a decline in memory, cognitive functions, and the ability to perform daily tasks. Named after Alois Alzheimer, who first described the condition in 1906, Alzheimer's is the most common cause of dementia among older adults, accounting for approximately 60-80% of all cases.
Causes and Risk Factors:

While the exact cause of Alzheimer's disease remains unclear, it is believed to result from a combination of genetic, environmental, and lifestyle factors. Mutations in certain genes, such as the APP, PSEN1, and PSEN2 genes, have been linked to the familial form of the disease, which accounts for a small percentage of cases. However, the majority of Alzheimer's cases are sporadic, meaning they develop without a clear familial link.

Age is the most significant risk factor for Alzheimer's, with the risk of developing the disease increasing with advancing age. Other risk factors include a family history of Alzheimer's, prior head injuries, cardiovascular diseases, hypertension, diabetes, and a sedentary lifestyle.

PATHOPHYSIOLOGY:

In Alzheimer's disease, two hallmark abnormalities are observed in the brain: the accumulation of amyloid-beta plaques and the formation of neurofibrillary tangles. Amyloid-beta is a protein fragment that aggregates and forms plaques, while neurofibrillary tangles consist of misfolded tau protein, leading to the disruption of the neuronal transport system. These abnormalities interfere with the communication between neurons and cause their gradual degeneration, resulting in cognitive decline and memory loss.

Stages and Symptoms:

Alzheimer's disease typically progresses through several stages, each with distinct symptoms:

1. **Preclinical Stage:** In this early stage,
    individuals may show no apparent
    symptoms, but changes in the brain are
    already occurring.
2. **Mild Cognitive Impairment (MCI):**
    At this stage, mild memory lapses and
    cognitive difficulties become noticeable
    but do not significantly impair daily
    functioning. Although, developing
    Alzheimer's disease is not applicable to
    everyone with MCI.
3. **Mild Alzheimer's Disease:** Memory
    loss and cognitive impairment become
    more apparent, affecting daily tasks,
    such as problem-solving and
    communication. Individuals may
    experience confusion, get lost in familiar
    places, and have difficulty managing
    finances.
4. **Moderate Alzheimer's Disease:** In
    this stage, symptoms worsen, and
    individuals require more assistance with
    daily activities. They may have difficulty
    recognizing loved ones, experience
    mood swings, and exhibit behavioral
    changes.

5. **Severe Alzheimer's Disease**: At the final stage, individuals lose the ability to communicate and become completely dependent on caregivers for all aspects of daily living. Physical functions, such as walking and swallowing, are also affected.

DIAGNOSIS AND TREATMENT:

Diagnosing Alzheimer's disease is challenging, as there is no definitive test. Physicians rely on medical history, cognitive assessments, neurological examinations, and brain imaging to rule out other conditions and make a probable diagnosis.

Currently, there is no cure for Alzheimer's disease. Treatment focuses on managing symptoms, improving the quality of life, and providing support to patients and their families. Medications, such as cholinesterase inhibitors and memantine, may be prescribed to help alleviate cognitive symptoms and slow disease progression in some cases.

In recent years, research into Alzheimer's disease has expanded significantly, with ongoing efforts to find effective treatments and potential preventive measures. Lifestyle factors, such as regular physical exercise, mental stimulation, a healthy diet, and social engagement, have been suggested to contribute to brain health and may reduce the risk of developing Alzheimer's or delay its onset.

Caregiving and Support:

Alzheimer's disease profoundly affects not only the individuals diagnosed but also their families and caregivers. To care _for someone with

Alzheimer's disease is usually psychologically, physically and emotionally draining if the caregiver is not being checked. Support groups, respite care, and professional assistance can provide essential support and help caregivers manage the challenges that come with the disease.

In conclusion, Alzheimer's disease is a complex and devastating condition that poses significant challenges to both individuals and society. Further research, increased awareness, and improved caregiving resources are crucial in the fight against this debilitating disease.

CHAPTER FIVE

HOW EXERCISE CAN HELP TO PREVENT DEMENTIA:

Exercise has been shown to play a significant role in preventing dementia and promoting overall brain health. Comprehensive studies have indicated several mechanisms through which exercise can offer protection:

1. **Improved Blood Flow:** Regular physical activity enhances blood circulation, leading to better oxygen and nutrient delivery to the brain. This supports brain function and reduces the risk of cognitive decline.
2. **Neurotransmitter Balance:** Exercise helps regulate neurotransmitters, such as dopamine and serotonin, which are vital for mood regulation and cognitive functions. Balanced neurotransmitter levels contribute to improved memory and cognitive abilities.
3. **Neuroplasticity:** Physical activity stimulates neuroplasticity, the brain's ability to reorganize and form new neural connections. This can enhance cognitive reserve, making the brain more resilient against neurological diseases like dementia.
4. **Reduction of Risk Factors:** Exercise helps manage cardiovascular risk factors like hypertension, diabetes, and obesity. These conditions are linked to an increased risk of dementia, and exercise can reduce their impact on the brain.

5. **Decreased Inflammation:** Regular exercise reduces chronic inflammation, which can contribute to cognitive decline. Lower inflammation levels protect brain cells and support their proper functioning.

6. **Antioxidant Effects**: Exercise enhances the body's production of antioxidants, which combat oxidative stress. Oxidative stress can damage brain cells and contribute to dementia, but regular exercise helps mitigate this effect.

7. **Enhanced Brain-Derived Neurotrophic Factor (BDNF):** Exercise increases the production of BDNF, a protein that supports the growth and survival of brain cells. Higher BDNF levels have been associated with better cognitive function and reduced risk of dementia.

8. **Stress Reduction:** Physical activity helps alleviate stress, which can negatively impact brain health. Managing stress through exercise supports a healthier brain.

To maximize the preventive benefits, it's recommended to engage in a combination of aerobic exercises, strength training, and activities that promote balance and flexibility. The ideal exercise regimen should be tailored to an individual's fitness level, taking any health conditions into consideration. Regularity is key, as long-term commitment to exercise has been associated with the most significant cognitive benefits. As with any health-related advice, consulting with a healthcare professional before starting a new exercise routine is advisable.

CHAPTER SIX

BEST DIET TO THE BRAIN:

"Diet for the brain" refers to a set of dietary principles aimed at promoting brain health and cognitive function. A well-balanced and nutritious diet can significantly impact brain health, memory, concentration, and overall mental well-being. They are as follows:

1. **Omega-3 Fatty Acids**: These essential fats are crucial for brain function and can be found in fatty fish (salmon, mackerel, sardines), flaxseeds, chia seeds, and walnuts. Omega-3s support brain cell structure and communication.
2. **Antioxidants:** Foods rich in antioxidants help protect the brain from oxidative stress and inflammation. Vegetables and Fruits like spinach and berries, broccoli and kale are perfect sources of antioxidants.
3. **Healthy Fats:** Besides omega-3s, healthy fats like olive oil and avocados provide essential nutrients that support brain health and may reduce the risk of cognitive decline.
4. **Complex Carbohydrates**: Whole grains, legumes, and starchy vegetables provide a steady supply of glucose to the brain, which is its main energy source. This helps maintain mental focus and concentration.

5. **B Vitamins:** Foods rich in B vitamins, such as folate, B6, and B12, support brain health and play a role in the synthesis of neurotransmitters. Sources include leafy greens, beans, eggs, and fortified cereals.

6. **Protein:** Adequate protein intake is essential for neurotransmitter production. Include lean sources of protein like poultry, fish, beans, tofu, and low-fat dairy in your diet.

7. **Water:** Staying hydrated is vital for brain function. Drink enough water throughout the day to support cognitive performance.

8. **Limit Added Sugars and Processed Foods:** High sugar intake and processed foods can lead to inflammation and negatively affect brain health, therefore,go for sugars gotten naturally from plants and avoid industrial sugar for the benefit of the brain.

9. **Moderation**: Maintain a balanced approach to eating and portion control to prevent overeating and promote overall well-being.

10. **Mediterranean Diet:** The
Mediterranean diet, which emphasizes
fruits, vegetables, whole grains, nuts,
seeds, and olive oil, has been linked to
better cognitive function and a reduced
risk of cognitive decline.

In addition to a brain-healthy diet, regular physical activity, adequate sleep, stress management, and cognitive stimulation through activities like puzzles or learning new skills also contribute to overall brain health.

It's essential to consult with a healthcare professional or a registered dietitian to create a personalized diet plan based on individual health needs and goals.

CHAPTER SEVEN

CAN PILLS KEEP THE BRAIN IN GOOD WORKING CONDITION?

The concept of pills or medications to enhance brain function and maintain cognitive health has been an intriguing topic of research and speculation. While there are some existing medications that can help manage certain brain-related conditions, such as Alzheimer's disease or attention deficit disorders, the idea of a single "brain pill" to optimize brain function and keep it in good working condition is still largely speculative.

Research into cognitive enhancers, also known as nootropics, has gained attention in recent years. These substances are believed to have the potential to improve cognitive abilities, memory, concentration, and overall brain health. Some common examples of nootropics include certain vitamins, herbal supplements, and pharmaceutical drugs like modafinil and piracetam.

However, it's important to note that the effectiveness and safety of many cognitive enhancers are still subjects of ongoing research and debate. While some studies suggest potential benefits, there are also concerns about potential side effects, long-term consequences, and ethical implications of using such substances.

The brain is an incredibly complex organ, and its health and performance depend on various factors, including genetics, lifestyle choices, diet, exercise, mental stimulation, and overall health. Taking a pill alone cannot replace the importance of a healthy lifestyle in maintaining brain function.

For individuals seeking to enhance cognitive function and maintain brain health, there are evidence-based approaches that can be beneficial. These include:

1. **Regular Exercise:** Physical activity has been shown to improve brain health and cognitive function, promoting the growth of new brain cells and enhancing overall brain plasticity.
2. **Balanced Diet:** Consuming a nutritious diet rich in antioxidants, omega-3 fatty acids, and other brain-boosting nutrients can support brain health and cognitive function.
3. **Mental Stimulation**: Engaging in activities that challenge the brain, such as puzzles, reading, learning new skills, and social interactions, can help maintain cognitive abilities.
4. **Sufficient Sleep:** Quality sleep is crucial for memory consolidation and overall brain function. Ensuring adequate rest is essential for optimal brain health.
5. **Stress Management:** Severe stress imposed on the brain can be lethal. Practicing relaxation techniques like meditation or mindfulness can be beneficial.

6. **Social Engagement**: Maintaining social connections and being part of a community can positively impact brain health.

In conclusion, while the idea of a pill to keep the brain in good working condition is an appealing notion, the reality is far more complex. Research into cognitive enhancers is ongoing, and it is crucial to approach such substances with caution, adhering to evidence-based practices and emphasizing lifestyle factors that promote brain health. Always consult with healthcare professionals before starting any new supplement or medication.

CHAPTER EIGHT

GETTING DEPRESSED?

Dementia is a broad term used to describe a group of cognitive disorders characterized by a decline in memory, thinking, reasoning, and the ability to perform daily activities.
 It can be a challenging condition for both individuals experiencing it and their loved ones.

Depression often coexists with dementia, and

here are some REASONS:

1. **Loss of Independence**: As dementia progresses, individuals may struggle to perform routine tasks independently, leading to a sense of helplessness and frustration, which can contribute to feelings of depression.

2. **Memory Loss and Cognitive Decline:** Memory impairment and difficulty with cognitive tasks can cause distress and anxiety, making it harder to cope with the changes that dementia brings.

3. **Social Isolation**: Dementia can result in social withdrawal, as individuals may feel embarrassed or overwhelmed by their condition. This feeling of rejection can arouse the need for solitude which can eventually birth depression.

4. **Grief and Loss:** Both the person with dementia and their loved ones experience a sense of loss as the disease affects relationships, abilities, and memories.

5. **Biological Factors:** Dementia can alter brain chemistry, which may contribute to depressive symptoms.

6. **Lack of Understanding:**
   Misunderstandings about dementia and
   the associated stigma can lead to
   feelings of shame and sadness in
   individuals with the condition.

It's crucial to seek professional help if you or someone you know is experiencing depression related to dementia. A healthcare provider can assess the situation, provide appropriate treatment, and offer support to manage both the dementia and the depression effectively.

Support groups, counseling, and involving family members in caregiving can also make a significant difference in managing the emotional impact of dementia. Encouraging engaging activities, maintaining a healthy lifestyle, and focusing on the person's remaining abilities can improve their overall well-being.

Endeavor to seek medical help and don't suffer in silence. Reach out to healthcare professionals, support networks, and resources available to help you navigate the challenges that come with dementia and depression.

CHAPTER NINE

SEEK MEDICAL EVALUATION:

If you or a loved one suspect that you might be suffering from dementia, seeking a comprehensive medical evaluation is essential. Dementia is a term used to describe a range of cognitive impairments that affect memory, thinking, and behavior. It is not a specific disease but rather a collection of symptoms caused by various underlying conditions. The most common cause of dementia is Alzheimer's disease, but other conditions such as vascular dementia, Lewy body dementia, frontotemporal dementia, and others can also lead to similar symptoms.

Here are the steps to take before going for a checkup if you suspect dementia:

1. **Recognize the Signs**: The first step is to be aware of the signs and symptoms of dementia. These may include memory loss, difficulty with language and communication, confusion, impaired judgment, mood changes, and difficulty performing everyday tasks.

2. **Consult Your Primary Care Physician**: If you or your family notice these symptoms, start by scheduling an appointment with your primary care physician. They can conduct a preliminary assessment, review your medical history, and perform basic cognitive tests.

3. **Specialist Referral:** Depending on the initial evaluation, your primary care physician may refer you to a specialist, such as a neurologist, geriatrician, or neuropsychologist, who has expertise in diagnosing and managing dementia.

4. **Comprehensive Evaluation**: The specialist will conduct a comprehensive evaluation, which may include a thorough medical history, cognitive tests, neurological examination, blood tests, brain imaging (e.g., MRI or CT scan), and sometimes lumbar puncture (spinal tap) to rule out other possible causes of cognitive impairment.
5. **Medical History and Symptoms:** During the evaluation, the doctor will inquire about your medical history, family history of dementia, and details about the symptoms you've been experiencing.
6. **Cognitive Testing:** Various tests will be administered to assess memory, attention, language, problem-solving skills, and other cognitive functions.
7. **Neurological Examination:** The doctor will perform a neurological examination to check for any physical signs of brain abnormalities.
8. **Brain Imaging:** Brain imaging, such as MRI or CT scan, can help identify brain changes associated with different types of dementia and exclude other conditions that might mimic dementia.

9. **Blood Tests:** Blood tests can help identify underlying medical conditions that might contribute to cognitive decline, such as vitamin deficiencies, thyroid problems, or infections.

10. **Lumbar Puncture (Spinal Tap):** In certain cases, a lumbar puncture may be recommended to analyze cerebrospinal fluid for signs of neurodegenerative disorders.

11. **Patient and Caregiver Input:** The evaluation may also involve gathering information from family members or caregivers to gain insights into the progression of symptoms and their impact on daily life.

12. **Diagnosis and Treatment Plan:** Once all the assessments are completed, the specialist will provide a diagnosis and discuss appropriate treatment options. Early diagnosis is crucial, as some types of dementia may have reversible causes or can benefit from intervention to slow down the progression.

13. **Post-Diagnosis Support:** After the diagnosis, your healthcare team will work with you and your family to create a personalized care plan, including medication management, lifestyle modifications, and support services to help cope with the challenges of dementia.

Remember, the process of diagnosing dementia can be complex, and not all memory problems indicate dementia. Sometimes, cognitive issues can be caused by medication side effects, depression, anxiety, or other treatable conditions. Seeking professional help is essential to ensure accurate diagnosis and appropriate management. Early detection can lead to better outcomes and improve the quality of life for both the person with dementia and their caregivers.

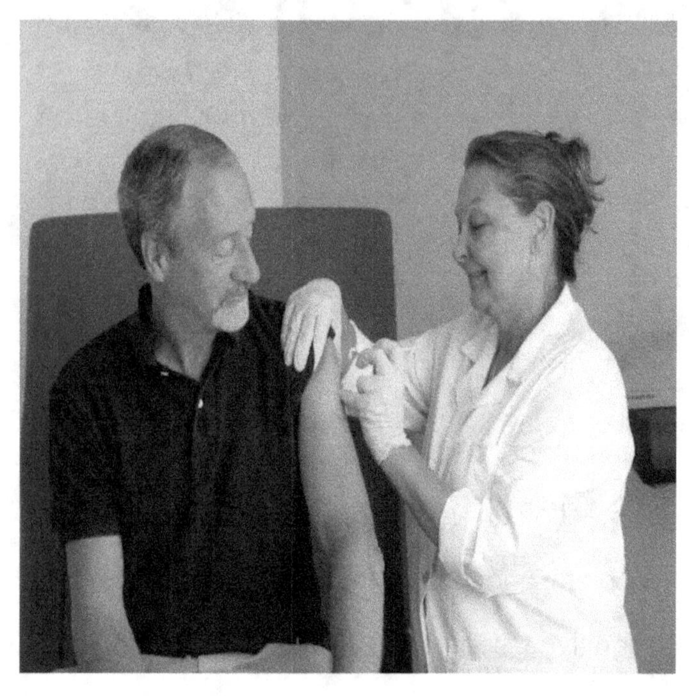

CHAPTER TEN

PRACTICE GOOD SLEEP ROUTINE

Practicing a consistent and healthy sleep schedule is essential for overall well-being, and it may play a significant role in reducing the risk of developing dementia. While there is no guaranteed way to prevent dementia, several studies suggest that adopting good sleep habits can be beneficial. In this comprehensive guide, I'll cover various strategies to help you practice a sleep schedule that may help in potentially reducing the risk of dementia:

1. **Understand the Importance of Sleep:** Recognize that sleep is a vital process for your brain to rest, repair, and consolidate memories. Adequate sleep is crucial for cognitive function and emotional well-being.

2. **Get a Timer for Your Sleep Schedule:** be consistent in flowing with your timer clock for your body to get used to. This helps regulate your body's internal clock, known as the circadian rhythm, which is closely linked to sleep quality.

3. **Have a Comfortable Bedtime Routine**: Establish a consistent and comfortable routine before bedtime for your body to adapt to it. Activities like reading a book, meditating, or taking a warm bath can promote relaxation and better sleep.

4. **Limit Daytime Naps**: While short power naps can be beneficial, excessive daytime sleep can disrupt your nighttime sleep. Keep naps to a maximum of 20-30 minutes and avoid napping too close to bedtime.

5. **Manage Exposure to Light:** Light exposure can affect your circadian rhythm. During the day, get natural sunlight, and in the evening, reduce exposure to bright screens, such as smartphones and tablets, as the blue light emitted can interfere with your ability to fall asleep.

6. **Be Mindful of Diet and Exercise:** Regular physical activity and a balanced diet can positively impact your sleep and overall brain health. Avoid heavy meals and caffeine close to bedtime, as they may disrupt your sleep patterns.

7. **Limit Alcohol and Nicotine:** Both alcohol and nicotine can negatively affect sleep quality. Try to limit or avoid their consumption, especially in the hours leading up to bedtime.

8. **Make your Sleep Environment Friendly:** Ensure that your bedroom is set up in such a way that it makes you enjoy comfort, quietness and the benefits that come with good sleep and remember to make your mattress and pillows enticing and fragranced.

9. **Manage Stress and Anxiety:** Chronic stress and anxiety can lead to sleep disturbances and potentially increase the risk of cognitive decline. Practice relaxation techniques such as deep breathing, yoga, or mindfulness to manage stress.

10. **Seek Medical Attention for Sleep Disorders**: If you experience persistent sleep problems, such as insomnia or sleep apnea, consult a healthcare professional. Tackling sleep disorders can be positively rewarding and impactful on the entirety of your health.

11. **Stay Mentally and Socially Active**: Engaging in cognitive activities, social interactions, and hobbies can keep your brain active and may help protect against dementia.

Remember, while following a healthy sleep schedule may reduce the risk of dementia, it's just one piece of the puzzle. Other factors such as genetics, lifestyle choices, and overall health play essential roles. Always consult with a healthcare professional for personalized advice and to address any specific concerns you may have about dementia or sleep-related issues.

CHAPTER ELEVEN

ANALYSIS OF GENDER DIFFERENCES ON DEMENTIA:

While there are similarities in the manifestation of dementia between men and women, there are also notable differences in prevalence, risk factors, and progression.

1. **Prevalence:** Studies suggest that women have a higher prevalence of dementia compared to men. This could be partially attributed to the longer life expectancy of women, as age is a significant risk factor for developing dementia.
2. **Risk Factors:** Both men and women share some common risk factors for dementia, such as age, family history, and genetics. However, certain risk factors may impact each gender differently. For example, cardiovascular

risk factors like high blood pressure and cholesterol may have a stronger association with dementia in men.

3. **Types of Dementia:** Alzheimer's disease is the most common form of dementia in both genders. However, some studies indicate that women may be more susceptible to Alzheimer's, while men may have a slightly higher risk of developing other types of dementia, like vascular dementia.

4. **Cognitive Decline:** Although the overall pattern of cognitive decline is similar in men and women with dementia, some studies suggest that women may experience more severe cognitive impairment in the early stages of the disease.

5. **Psychosocial Aspects**: The experience of dementia can also differ between men and women due to societal norms and gender roles. Women often bear a higher caregiving burden as they are more likely to be caregivers for family members with dementia.

6. **Hormonal Influences:** Hormonal changes throughout a woman's

life, such as during menopause, may play a role in cognitive decline and dementia risk. However, the next chapter gives more analysis on why women are mostly affected by dementia.

NOTE: While dementia affects both men and women, there are differences in prevalence, risk factors, and cognitive patterns between the genders. Understanding these distinctions can lead to better-tailored prevention strategies, treatment approaches, and support for individuals and their families affected by dementia.

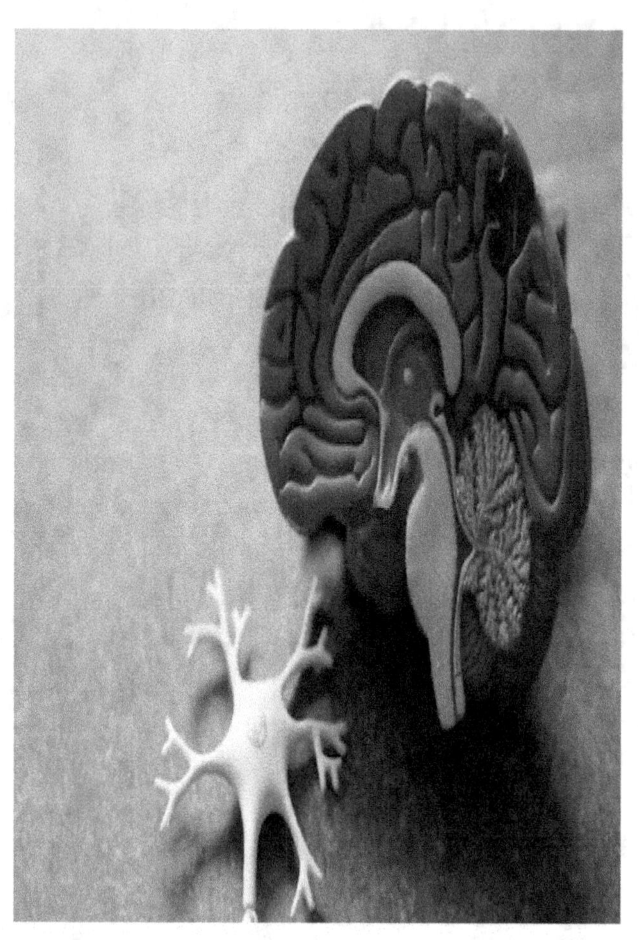

CHAPTER TWELVE

WHY WOMEN ARE HIGHLY AFFECTED:

While it is true that women are more affected by dementia compared to men, the reasons for this disparity are multifactorial and complex. Various biological, hormonal, genetic, and social factors contribute to the higher prevalence of dementia in women. Here is an extensive and comprehensive explanation of some key factors:

1. **Hormonal Differences**: Estrogen, the primary female sex hormone, has been shown to have a neuroprotective effect on the brain. During menopause, women experience a significant decline in estrogen levels, which may leave them more vulnerable to cognitive decline and dementia.
2. **Longer Lifespan**: Women generally have longer lifespans than men. Since dementia risk increases with age, the higher life expectancy of women means they have more years during which they can develop dementia.
3. **Genetics:** Some genetic factors are associated with an increased risk of developing dementia. The apolipoprotein E (APOE) gene, specifically the APOE-ε4 allele, is a significant genetic risk factor for Alzheimer's disease, the most common form of dementia. Studies have suggested that women may have a higher prevalence of this genetic risk factor compared to men.

4. **Cardiovascular Health:**
   Cardiovascular risk factors such as
   hypertension, diabetes, and high
   cholesterol are linked to an increased
   risk of dementia. Women tend to have a
   higher prevalence of certain
   cardiovascular risk factors, which could
   contribute to their higher dementia risk.

5. **Social and Lifestyle Factors:**
   Women often take on caregiving roles
   for family members with dementia,
   leading to increased stress and potential
   negative impacts on their own health.
   Additionally, certain lifestyle choices,
   such as diet, exercise, and education,
   can influence dementia risk, and these
   factors may vary between genders.

6. **Underdiagnosis in Men:** Dementia
   symptoms can manifest differently in
   men and women. Men may be more
   likely to exhibit aggressive or disruptive
   behaviors, leading to a higher likelihood
   of being diagnosed with other
   conditions, such as depression or
   behavioral disorders, instead of
   dementia.

7. **Cerebrovascular Differences:** Some studies suggest that women may have a higher incidence of cerebrovascular disease, such as small vessel disease, which can contribute to cognitive impairment and vascular dementia.

8. **Neurobiological Differences:** Research has shown that male and female brains differ in their structure and function, which may influence the susceptibility to various neurological conditions, including dementia.

9. **Estrogen Replacement Therapy:** While estrogen has been associated with neuroprotective effects, the use of hormone replacement therapy (HRT) to alleviate menopause symptoms has shown mixed results regarding its impact on dementia risk. Some studies have suggested a potential protective effect, while others have raised concerns about increased risk when HRT is started later in life.

10. **Research Bias:** Historically, clinical trials and studies on dementia have disproportionately included male participants, which might have led to a better understanding of dementia risk factors in men than in women.

It's important to note that the interplay of these factors is highly complex, and more research is needed to fully understand the underlying mechanisms behind the gender disparity in dementia. Addressing the issue requires a comprehensive approach that considers biological, genetic, social, and lifestyle factors, aiming to improve preventive strategies and provide better support and care for those affected by dementia, regardless of gender.

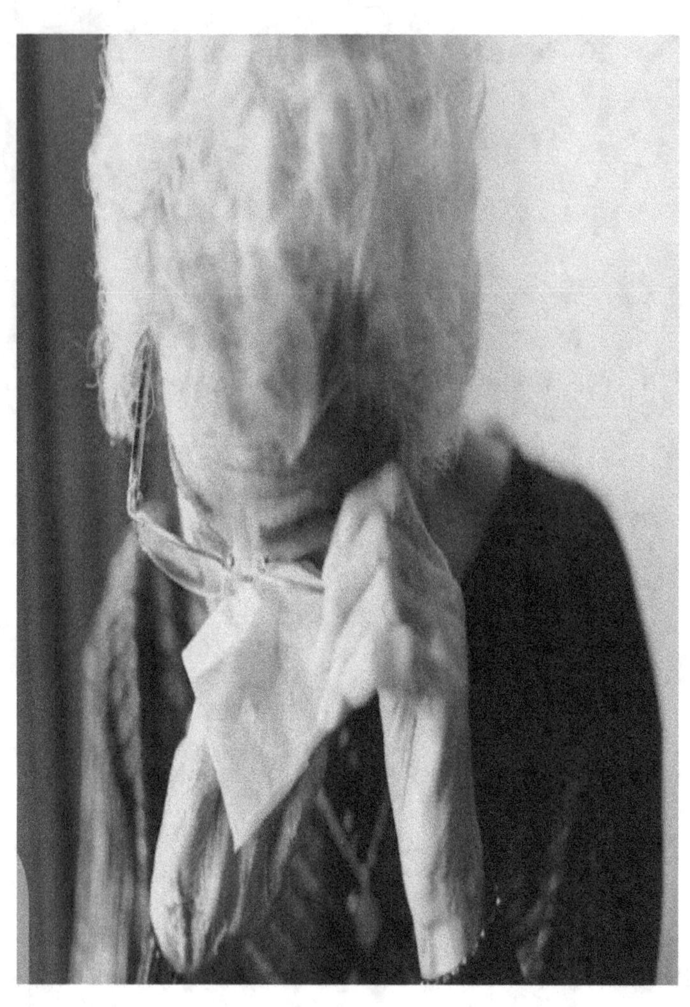

CHAPTER THIRTEEN

DUTIES OF DEMENTIA EXPERTS

Experts on dementia play a crucial role in supporting individuals with dementia and their caregivers. Their duties encompass a wide range of responsibilities, including assessment, diagnosis, treatment, education, and research. Here are some key areas where their expertise is applied:

1. **Assessment and Diagnosis:**
    Dementia experts are trained to conduct
    thorough assessments to diagnose
    dementia accurately. They evaluate
    cognitive abilities, memory, language,
    behavior, and other relevant factors to
    determine the type and stage of
    dementia a person may have.
2. **Treatment Planning**: Once a
    diagnosis is made, dementia experts
    collaborate with patients and their
    caregivers to develop personalized
    treatment plans. These plans may
    include medication management,
    cognitive stimulation therapies, lifestyle
    modifications, and strategies to manage
    behavioral symptoms.
3. **Education and Support:** Dementia
    experts play an essential role in
    educating patients and their families
    about the condition. They provide
    information on disease progression,
    coping strategies, and ways to enhance
    the quality of life for those living with
    dementia.

4. **Caregiver Training**: Supporting caregivers is a crucial aspect of dementia care. Experts offer training to caregivers, helping them understand the challenges associated with dementia and equipping them with the skills to provide appropriate care and support.

5. **Psychological Support:** Dementia can take an emotional toll on both patients and caregivers. Experts offer psychological support to help individuals cope with the stress, anxiety, and depression that may accompany the disease.

6. **Medication Management:** Dementia experts are knowledgeable about various medications used to manage dementia symptoms. They monitor patients' responses to medications and make adjustments as needed.

7. **Research and Clinical Trials:** Many dementia experts are involved in research to advance knowledge about dementia causes, treatments, and potential cures. They may participate in clinical trials to test new therapies and interventions.

8. **Promoting Independence:** Dementia
    experts work with patients to promote
    independence for as long as possible.
    They develop strategies to enhance
    daily living skills and support autonomy
    while ensuring safety.

9. **Advocacy and Policy
    Development:** Some experts on
    dementia are actively involved in
    advocating for better policies and
    resources to support individuals with
    dementia and their families. They work
    to raise awareness and reduce stigma
    surrounding the condition.

10. **Community Engagement:** Dementia
    experts often engage with the
    community to educate the public about
    dementia, early warning signs, and the
    importance of seeking early diagnosis
    and intervention.

11. **End-of-life Care:** Dementia experts
    support patients and their families in
    making end-of-life decisions and
    ensuring that their wishes are
    respected.

Overall, the duties of dementia experts extend beyond clinical care to include comprehensive support for patients and their caregivers, research contributions, advocacy efforts, and community outreach to create a more dementia-friendly society. Their expertise is vital in improving the lives of those affected by this challenging condition.

CONCLUSION

In conclusion, dementia is a complex and debilitating neurological condition that poses significant challenges to affected individuals, their families, and society at large. Throughout this discussion, we have explored the various aspects of dementia, including its definition, causes, symptoms, and impact on individuals' cognitive and functional abilities.

As our understanding of dementia continues to evolve, it becomes increasingly crucial to raise awareness about the condition and invest in research and support services. Early diagnosis and interventions can improve the quality of life for those living with dementia and their caregivers, enabling them to better cope with the challenges they face.

Furthermore, we have seen that the burden of dementia extends beyond the individual to encompass the emotional, financial, and societal implications. Adequate resources and a compassionate approach are essential to ensure that individuals with dementia receive the care and dignity they deserve.

Promising advancements in medical research and innovative therapies offer hope for potential treatments and prevention strategies in the future. However, it remains vital to prioritize public health initiatives that promote brain health, early detection, and lifestyle interventions that may reduce the risk of dementia.

Ultimately, addressing the issue of dementia requires a comprehensive and collaborative effort involving governments, healthcare providers, researchers, caregivers, and communities. By fostering understanding, empathy, and support, we can strive towards a world where dementia is met with compassion and effective solutions, empowering individuals and families to live fulfilling lives despite the challenges posed by this condition.

www.ingramcontent.com/pod-product-compliance
Lightning Source LLC
Chambersburg PA
CBHW070953250726
48663CB00002B/205